This Journal Belongs To:

Maddie Bowers ♥ Ü

Very Private ♥ Ü

NOt Private any more ♡ Ü

I have been writing fictional and non-fictional stories and I am enjoying it. I am 10 and its the 27th December, 2021 ♥ Christmas is over and I need to start taking my hobby more seriously now. Talk to you later guys ♥ ☺

Cooking, writing, walking the dog, playing golf, having fun with my BFFs Erica, Ewan, Indie, Vivi, Esme, Ava. and and george Georgia ☺

There are many things I would like to acomplish this year. I would like to acheive to get below 35 in my handy cap (hopefully) ☺
I want to play more netball.
I am really enjoying that. It makes me feel like I can control what I want to do and no one is in charge of me. Just like my gols ☺

I might want to get my own hoop sor net ball. or get a net sor gols to put. Im thinking to go and play gols everyday. I dont think that will happen ☺

~~I also wanted my~~ I also want to do more compoticions in gols. I want to WIN!!!!!!!!!(!)
Also I really want to ~~s~~ sspend more time with emma because we ~~havett~~ havent talked much n We are still BFFFFFF'S ☺ Now on to my real Journal!

Saturday 12th febuary 2022
10:38am Currently. What I am doing:
We are getting ready to go out
for a very fancy lunch with our
friends. We are going to have so
much sweets ~~can~~ I can't wait
to see my BFF! I just came out
~~of~~. of the bye!

Just got back from my grandreas
from a 2 hour ~~~~ journey

So tierd ;;
So late. it 9:40pm Im nearly
ready for bed ⛑ ~~~~ ŭ bye ŭ

Guys, I am going to an epic party tonight with my whole class and all of my friends and the boys too

NOTES & REMINDERS:

your pretty

My dog is the most
exciting part of
my life

THOUGHTS & IDEAS: My holiday is gonna be
amazing! :) yasssssss

HAV YOU SO

NOTES & REMINDERS:

Your Pretty

THOUGHTS & IDEAS:

NOTES & REMINDERS:

your really pretty

♥

your really pretty

♥

THOUGHTS & IDEAS: U Yass queens

Holiday specials! w m

m . Dont you want

Math problems to party U?

IM so exicted!

NOTES & REMINDERS:

your really pretty
♥

your really pretty
♥

your really pretty

THOUGHTS & IDEAS:

NOTES & REMINDERS:

your really pretty

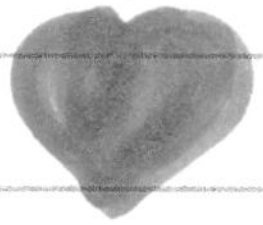

Slay!

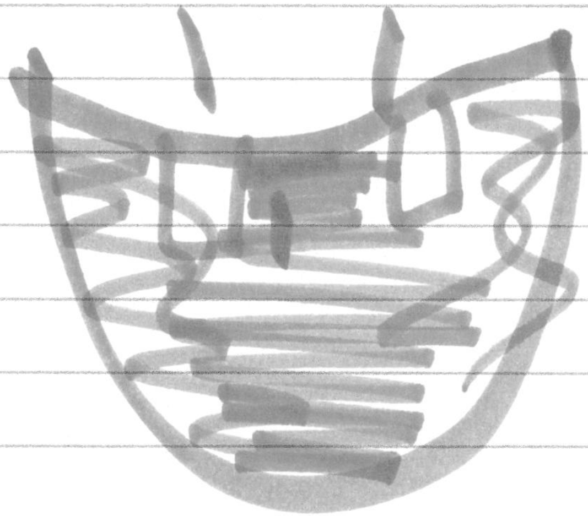

THOUGHTS & IDEAS:

_____

_____

_____

_____

_____

_____

_____

_____

_____

_____

_____

_____

_____

NOTES & REMINDERS:

THOUGHTS & IDEAS:

NOTES & REMINDERS:

THOUGHTS & IDEAS:

NOTES & REMINDERS:

THOUGHTS & IDEAS:

_____

_____

_____

_____

_____

_____

_____

_____

_____

_____

_____

_____

_____

_____

NOTES & REMINDERS:

THOUGHTS & IDEAS:

_____

_____

_____

_____

_____

_____

_____

_____

_____

_____

_____

_____

_____

_____

NOTES & REMINDERS:

THOUGHTS & IDEAS:

_____

_____

_____

_____

_____

_____

_____

_____

_____

_____

_____

_____

_____

NOTES & REMINDERS:

THOUGHTS & IDEAS:

NOTES & REMINDERS:

THOUGHTS & IDEAS:

_____

_____

_____

_____

_____

_____

_____

_____

_____

_____

_____

_____

_____

_____

NOTES & REMINDERS:

THOUGHTS & IDEAS:

NOTES & REMINDERS:

THOUGHTS & IDEAS:

NOTES & REMINDERS:

THOUGHTS & IDEAS:

NOTES & REMINDERS:

THOUGHTS & IDEAS:

NOTES & REMINDERS:

THOUGHTS & IDEAS:

NOTES & REMINDERS:

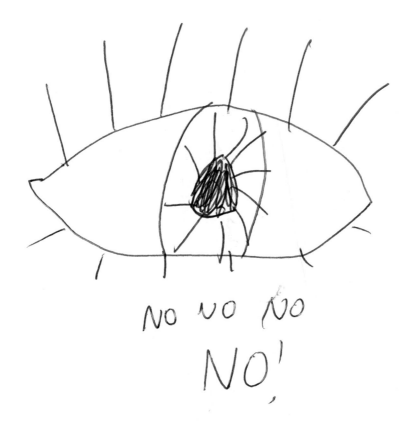

NO NO NO
NO!

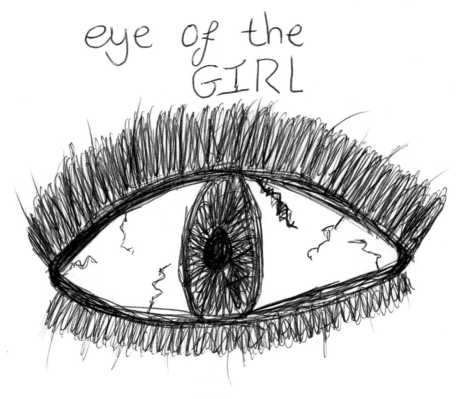

eye of the GIRL

Printed in Great Britain
by Amazon